GW01086581

THE BOOKING AGENT'S BOOK OF SECRETS FOR

TOURING
MUSICIANS

(or, a step-by-step guide to getting an agent,
and doing the job yourself in the meantime)

PHIL SIMPSON

Dedicated to Jessica and Rupert.

Table of Contents

Author's Note

Please note that everything in this book is written from my own personal and professional experience in the industry; take the points in this book as guidance, not necessarily recommendation, and know that there will always be different approaches to some of the methods I lay out here. These strategies might not work for everyone, but I hope that you find it useful to hear my take and all that I have learnt from my ten-plus years' experience as a booking agent.

If you're an artist reading this book, note that it is written with the assumption you're reading it with a desire to further develop your touring career, and increase your profile. If you have no interest in this side of it and just wish to perform whenever, wherever, and to whoever will have you, there is a good chance this book might not be for you. My aim is to climb you to the summit via the shortest and most-efficient route, as opposed to taking the contour trail of the Sunday rambler.

Though this is very much a workbook (and you should feel able to dip in and out at your leisure), to get the most from it I would encourage you to enjoy the book in its entirety before implementing any of the steps outlined.

I mostly speak from a UK perspective throughout, but do note the principles are generally the same the world over.

Introduction

Welcome, and thank you for buying this book.

I've been a booking agent in the UK for over ten years now. Though I've seen countless success stories (and I'll be forever grateful for having played a role in these), I've also seen many artists who have had a real chance and blown it; sometimes from arrogance or apathy, but most often from simple inexperience.

One of the most frustrating things about being an agent is the fact that you just can't help everyone. There is so much amazing music out there, but so little time.

If I had time to advise just a third of those who came to me for help, I'd feel like I was making a difference. That's why I put together this book.

It's time to lift the lid on the mysterious world of booking agents.

In this book, I reveal all about what we do and how we do it. You'll find guidance on negotiating not just the deals, but the sometimes-nefarious world of the music industry, and I even let you in on my 4-point plan on how to get an agent.

In Part 1, you'll learn the basics about booking agents and how to get one, and in Part 2, you'll learn how to be your own booking agent in the meantime, with the benefit of all the insider 'thinking like an agent' tips I lay out for you.

Good luck on your journey.

Phil Simpson
May 2020

Part 1: Understanding Agents

Chapter 1: What is an Agent and What do They do?

In the most basic terms, a booking agent is responsible for coordinating an artist's live career.

As the exclusive representative of the artist, the agent works closely with the act and their team to plan and book their live schedule.

It's not just a case of sourcing work; an agent's responsibility is to ensure they're pitching their artists for all the appropriate opportunities such as high-profile festivals and shows, support slots that could be beneficial to their careers, showcases, and private events.

Agents should represent their artists comprehensively; regularly reflecting their artists' plans and achievements to potential bookers, protecting their value in the market, and negotiating on their behalf to get the best fees.

Once engagements are confirmed, legally binding contracts are issued, and the shows are seen through to completion. Agents are also often responsible for coordinating immigration clearances, informing artists of tax liabilities (and/or filling out waivers), and mediating disputes where necessary.

An agent makes their money by taking a percentage of the artist's gross (before any expenses) fee per performance—in most cases between 10-20%. You are paying an agent for not only their skills in booking but also for their contacts, experience, and influence.

A good agent will have an extensive list of contacts from across the live spectrum (nationwide, and globally). I might add this isn't just a literal list; there will be personal relationships behind many of them—agents are very well-connected networkers.

Though individual agents' jobs day-to-day are mostly the same, the umbrellas above them can differ greatly; there are many agents that are part of big conglomerate agencies (representing hundreds of artists and having offices in every continent), but there are also plenty that are part of smaller independent agencies or are sole operators. From an artist's perspective, there are advantages and disadvantages with all, but my tip would be to always think of who your actual day-to-day agent is/will be; who they also work with, what the fit feels like, and importantly, whether you 'click' as people. These are often much more important factors than the name above their office door.

Some things booking agents don't do:

- A good agent doesn't just wait for the phone to ring; they identify opportunities and go after them.

- Although they certainly have an interest in it, agents generally don't promote the shows. This is the responsibility of the promoter or talent buyer.

- Though any agent will do their best to increase a band's profile, an agent can't make their artist the next big thing overnight. At any level, this takes time.

- Most agents won't organise things like international transport or hotels. This would normally be the job of the artist or their management.

- Most agents won't get involved artistically with the artist, although they'll often be consulted and privy to early work.

- Unlike some areas of the business, agents don't give advances. They get paid when the artist does (when the gig has happened).

Most agents represent specific areas/continents/countries. UK agents usually book for Europe, and in the US, agents frequently book for Canada as well. No agreement is the same though, and you can have UK agents that book Europe except from the Netherlands, Belgium, and Luxembourg (BeNeLux), or that only book the UK & Ireland, for example. It very much comes down to which territories the agent's areas of expertise lies in, and which have been agreed on as part of the deal at the time of signing.

The term 'signing' in our context generally means starting a working relationship, and though many agents have contracts with their artists, some do not. It's important to remember the agent is appointed by the artist, and so works for the artist. Many agents deem a contractual commitment or minimum term unnecessary; as long as the agent works hard, and the relationship remains strong, the artist should have no reason to leave. Keeping hold of their artists (and thus reputation) provides great motivation for the agent to do a good job.

No day is ever really the same for an agent. Mine is usually spent mostly on the phone, but also on email, chatting with concert promoters and festival organisers about the bands I work with. I might have a band currently on the road to which I'm monitoring the progress of the sales, or I might be discussing with my bands what their live strategy should be for the next eighteen months ahead. Days can be long, and it's hard when you face rejection, but any agent will tell you it's for the majority, extremely satisfying and rewarding work.

Key Takeaways from Chapter 1:

- An agent doesn't just get an artist work, but strategises their whole live career, binds engagements in law, and boasts an extensive list of contacts, most of whom they know on a personal level.

- An agent makes their money by taking a percentage cut of every show fee an artist gets.

- It's important to agree which territories an agent will cover at the time of 'signing'.

Chapter 2: What a Booking Agent Looks for in Potential New Artists

Getting a booking agent can be a difficult and time-consuming process. It rarely happens overnight.

Agents can't just be hired and are often elusive; rarely responding to unsolicited requests from acts (particularly from those they've never heard of).

We get lots of submissions.

And no matter what we tell you, **we're always looking for new artists**.

As an agent gets their cut from an artist's fee (which for concerts, comes from the money the artist generates from ticket sales), their whole model is built around trying to calculate which artists are either selling lots of tickets (nationwide or even internationally), or have the potential to.

It's often a bit of a chicken-and-egg situation, as most agents will want to see an already busy gig schedule, and some serious ticket-sales traction before getting involved. Many artists however don't know how to get to this point without an agent.

They may also want to see other parts of the industry already involved with the artist; a publicist, a manager perhaps, a record label, etc. But often, agents are one of the first to get involved with an artist, and once on board, can play a role in recruiting other members of an artist's team, in the hope that doing so will make their new signing an even more viable prospect.

Agents want their artists to be extremely hard-working. After all, they're going to be spending a large amount of time working very hard for them, so if they can see an artist is lacking drive (ambition is infectious!), a head for business, or the essential communication and people skills necessary, they're unlikely to be interested. If they can see the artist has been booking their tours themselves for the last couple of years (and good tours they are!) and has a solid fanbase they're actively engaging with, this will impress them.

Most agents will want to fall in love with the music they're working with. My personal belief is the success of artists mostly lies with the music they create. Even though an agent's interest is very much in the live show, audiences won't come out time and time again unless the artist they are going out to see is creating fantastic music that touches them in some way. You can be the best live band in the world, but if you've not left the audience affected, or humming the tune *'I just have to hear that song again'* on the way home, you have not connected on the longevity scale. As an artist, you want your representative to completely 'get' what you do, be enthusiastic and passionate about selling you, and share in your ambition and aims for the future.

But ultimately, **an agent is out to make a living**. There will never be a shortage of artists looking for agents, but only a small fraction of artists exist in the sweet spot where they're starting to make some serious traction (and money) but are not yet represented by an agent.

How Agents Find Artists

Note, it's usually that way around.

The truth is, not many agents randomly 'go looking' for artists. They're too busy.

'Far too busy to take on anyone else right now.'

Or that's at least what they might say until the *right* act comes along.

The most frequent way an agent signs an artist is when the agent is approached directly by the management of an artist.

Managers and agents work very closely, usually speaking daily, and often socialising outside of work. Trust and friendships build up, and it's very common for managers to manage maybe five or six artists, and have the same agent booking the majority of them. This is because a) the agent knows the management (whose opinion they trust, and whom they get on with) and b), they can make a safe assumption that big things will happen for the artist in question, just like it has for all the other artists the manager works with.

This scenario is also common because in the eyes of the agent, if an artist is working with a manager, there is someone else already involved helping to drive things forward—arguably more than the artist might otherwise be able to do on their own.

Another way agents find artists is by recommendation; someone they know well and trust in the business has tipped them off. Often, there might be more than one 'tipper', and there will be a 'buzz' building up about the artist.

Even then, that might not be enough to make an agent make a move. I've often been in this situation personally. I've gone along to a gig (bought a ticket as I didn't want the band to know I was there and find myself in a potentially awkward situation!), been less than impressed, and walked away.

Or, the said agent might genuinely be too busy. It then goes around again until someone else makes a recommendation and so on.

As I mentioned earlier, agents get relentless approaches from artists, and although many are discarded, occasionally the agent might have already heard something about the artist, has maybe seen them at a festival, or has some evidence or experience with the band doing the unsolicited approach. It's rare that an agent might take on an artist in this way, but it does happen.

One of the most common movements between artists and agents is when an artist's team changes. Often the artist already has an agent, but the artist might get a new manager who comes in and appoints a whole new team—including agent—**because they like working with people they know and can trust.**

Key Takeaways from Chapter 2:

- Most often, agents find artists, not the other way around.

- Agents are always looking for new artists to work with.

- Networks often form the basis of how artists get representation.

- Managers are a good route to representation.

- People work with people they like and get on with.

- It's a given that the band has to be at the top of their game in the music they create, and the live show they put on.

Chapter 3:
Do I Need an Agent?

In short, yes. If you are serious about taking your career as far as it can go, you will at some point need an agent.

There are two main reasons for this:

Firstly, you will reach a point where you are too busy getting requests to play, that you simply won't have time to deal with them properly whilst doing all the important stuff like songwriting, releasing records, and actually gigging.

It's very easy to take your eye off the ball for the short-term buck and lose focus on what is actually driving the source of your income to start with: your music. If you are doing everything right, you will naturally reach a point where you become an attractive prospect to an agent.

Secondly, there will come a point in your career (though it could take a while before becoming apparent) where there will be some gigs you won't be able to get without an agent. If you have resisted or squandered this 'natural-selection' progression for whatever reason, you will lose out somewhere down the line and your growth will be stunted, whether you realise it or not.

This book is intended to get you to this point, whilst ensuring you understand the process well enough to do it yourself in the meantime, and be able to make an informed choice when the time does come.

Key Takeaways from Chapter 3:

- For your career to reach the highest possible level, you will at some point need an agent.

- Not only can you do most of the bookings yourself initially, but it is good practice to so that you fully understand the agent's role when the time comes to sign.

Chapter 4: My 4-Point Plan to Get an Agent

This does require work and you may not be able to be implement each point immediately, but if I had to summarise the quickest route to representation for an artist, it would be as follows.

I am not including things you should have in place that I would deem a 'given' such as:

- You are producing **excellent** music and present a polished live show.
- You have a well-written biography (no more than one page).
- You have at least four professionally shot hi-res press photos (not live).
- You have music available to purchase online.
- You have professional-quality videos (live and studio versions) on YouTube.
- You have profiles on Songkick, BandsinTown, Spotify, Ents24, etc.

1. Grow your audience online so that you're regularly achieving over three-thousand monthly listeners on Spotify (or similar), and have over three-thousand followers on two thirds of your social media accounts (Twitter, Facebook, Instagram).

2. Get to a point in your live career where you're gigging regularly and selling around a hundred tickets everywhere you play outside your hometown. In your hometown, the figure should be closer to three hundred.

3. Wait until you're about to enter a new album cycle; that is, you have (an excellent, 'your best') new album recorded, and are starting to put a plan together for the next eighteen months 'cycle'. Recruit a PR company/publicist who are 'ready to go' and get a smaller-than-usual London (or similar big-market-in-your-country) gig lined up for around six weeks' time on a Tuesday* night, with a cheap-list for your top fans.

4. Put a list together of ten suitable agents for your music (based on the bands they're currently booking) and ten suitable management companies (remember managers are great conduits to agents). There are some ideas below, but it's important you do your own research as well. Look at who your favourite acts are represented by for management and live work as a good starting point.

Examples of Booking Agencies:

Paradigm (Worldwide)
X-Ray Touring (Worldwide)
United Talent Agency (Worldwide)
ATC Live (UK)
Primary Talent (UK)
International Talent Booking (UK)
The Feldman Agency (North America)
Paquin Artists Agency (North America)

Examples of Music Management Companies:

The Music Manager's Forum (UK)
The Unsigned Guide (listings -UK)
ATC Management (UK)
Paquin Artists Management (CAN)
Big Noise (USA)

Brilliant Noise (USA)
Red Light Management (North America)

Now put a wow** pitch together to your 'top five' of each (agency and management) detailing:

1. Who you are and what you do.

2. An introduction to your music.

3. Your career highlights so far.

4. Ticket sales data (and how many you're selling in four markets including London/similar).

5. What festivals you've played.

6. Your new album plan, and plan for the next eighteen months —including the PR.

7. A request to go and meet them to chat about your plans, and that 'you'd love to have them involved'.

8. Invite them (+1 on the guest list) to the London gig.

The aim here should be to get face-to-face meetings with (at their offices), and attendance at your London gig (which you should work hard to sell out) from at least three agents and three managers.

It might take a few follow-up emails and calls, but be persistent. If you come to a dead-end, repeat the process from the remaining names on your list.

*In UK terms, Tuesday is a good night to play London. Wednesdays and Thursdays are better generally, but in this case, you want to minimise what competition you might have for getting the industry figures out. (they generally don't go to shows at weekends).

**a 'wow' pitch is the best email you've ever written. Ever. Persuasive yet friendly, factual yet brief.

Key Takeaways from Chapter 4:

- Ensure you have everything in place before starting to approach agents. You don't want to make a move too early.

- The focus should be on arranging meetings, and getting the agents and managers out to your shows.

- You don't ask, you don't get. Be persistent and exceedingly polite in your follow-ups.

- See this as a long process that requires early set up, ongoing follow-up whilst keeping them updated, and building up rapport. Be resilient and keep going.

Part 2: How to Be Your Own Booking Agent

Although you may be on the search for an agent, it's entirely possible for artists to do their own bookings, either in the meantime whilst courting an agent, or longer term.

You are more likely to get an agent (and be in a better place to evaluate your options) if you understand the role of an agent by doing it yourself for a while. In this section, we'll talk about the best way to go about this.

Whether you do want to just tide yourself over for now, or you actually want to be an agent full time, you'll learn all you need to know, from the basics of booking your own gigs, to learning how an agent thinks, to then actually heading out on tour and getting paid.

We will also touch on elements outside the agent's responsibilities, where the agent will often have a role in facilitating, but will not necessarily take the lead on.

Chapter 5: Taking on the Role Yourself

In this chapter, we'll get started in setting up your system, and also ensure you're up to speed on the different types of organisations you will be dealing with. We will then go on to look at creating your own database of venues, promoters, and festivals tailored to your music.

Networking

As we've already learnt, a good agent will be very well connected and will know many of the bookers and promoters well. Anyone wishing to be an agent should be focused on getting out and about and meeting as many of the relevant industry figures as possible.

A good way to do this quickly is at showcase festivals and conferences. Whilst hopefully getting a showcase yourself as an artist, you'll have the opportunity to learn more about the industry and meet a lot of the 'movers and shakers' working in it.

Usually based around a conference and networking event, showcase festivals allow artists to perform to industry delegates, often in a 'real life' gig scenario.

Attendance (and a showcase) at one of these events, should be an early aim for anyone serious about building their career in this field. I still attend at least five each year.

Even if you applied for a showcase at one and weren't successful, I'd still think about attending as a delegate as they are packed with useful 'roundtables', panel sessions, and of course, industry professionals.

Some example events from the UK:

Americana Music Association (UK) (London, January)
The Great Escape (Brighton, May)
Liverpool SoundCity (Liverpool, May)
Focus Wales (Wrexham, May)

And across the World:

Eurosonic Noorderslag (Netherlands, January)
APAP (USA, January)
SXSW (USA, March)
Reeperbahn (Germany, September)
Canadian Music Week (Canada, September)

Brand & Email

Firstly, I'm going to assume you already have a great website, a very active social media following (Facebook, Twitter, Instagram), some great videos on YouTube (a mixture of quality live and studio videos) and that you have music available to purchase and stream online. These are very much the basics.

I would recommend setting up a new email address for your bookings; something like:

management@yourband.com
bookings@yourband.com

Having a dedicated account solely for live bookings not only makes things easier for you, but it also looks good from the outside. It will be obvious you're not represented, but it gives the impression you are a bit more organised—rather than just using a generic (free) yourband@gmail.com account or similar.

Some bands opt to create a whole new brand/business name for their bookings, almost like a 'fake' agency. This is possible, but it could cause problems later down the line if you are ultimately seeking to be represented by an agent.

Regardless of where it comes from, you should have a good email signature with a one-liner about you/your music, a good quote, and your contact mobile number.

Your Booking System

A booking agent needs to be highly organised. I am often spinning many plates at any one time, with numerous tours to book, festival offers to confirm, and a multitude of other requests waiting to be actioned—for all of my twenty-one-strong roster of artists.

Professional agents of course have dedicated booking systems to keep track of things, but for now, we will go through the process of setting up a DIY system to keep you organised. It will be made up of the following:

1. A database of promoters, with details.
2. A database of venues, with details
3. A database of festivals, with details.
4. A planning spreadsheet where you can keep track of your actual date-booking

Things to Do Now 1:

Task 1:

Research and make a list of who you perceive to be the main concert promoters who organise shows in your genre. Venues often display who is presenting (promoting) the show on their listings. Once you have a name, look on their website for further details. Try searching Google for "presents:[band name]" [city] to find out who is promoting a certain show. Have a look on Facebook to find out who has created the event or is listed as a host. Search for the gig on Twitter—who has tweeted about it?

Put these into a spreadsheet titled 'Promoters'. At the end of this section you'll see a QR code which you can scan, and it will instantly take you to a private link on my website where you can download a free pack of example files for this section. Feel free to use these or create your own based on them.

Task 2:

Using any streaming/social media geographic/Google analytics website data you might have on where your fans are mostly located (you should be analysing this regularly anyway), identify thirty cities/towns in your country where you think you might have an audience, and should be playing.

Based on what you might know about the venues in these towns already, research to see where similar artists are playing and make a list of suitable venues. Try to have at least three venue options per town/city/area.

Put these into a new tab on your spreadsheet called 'venues', with the following headings:

TOWN, VENUE, CAPACITY, CONTACT, EMAIL ADDRESS, PHONE NUMBER, 1ST CONTACT DATE, 2ND CONTACT DATE, RESULT

Try to complete as much information as you can under the headings you've created. You are aiming to build up an ever-increasing database of venues, so you have all of this information in one place.

Ninety percent of the time you can find details such as venue capacities on venue' websites, or from some clever searching on Google. You are also likely to be able to find details of the venue booker's name, email address, and often, even mobile contact numbers. Anything you can find online in the public domain is fair game in my opinion.

This will be more of an ongoing task, but it's a great tool to get you learning more about the circuit and will allow you to plan your best possible tours. Keep it updated at all times and whenever you get a new nugget of information, add it in. This will be your new workspace.

Task 3:

Make a third tab on your spreadsheet just for festivals.

Start with twenty festivals you're certain your music would be a perfect fit for and begin researching details of the bookers/organisers. Again, you'll find more than you expect with some clever searching. Fill in their information as you get it. Keep this updated whenever you find out some new information about them.

Task 4:

Make up a progress spreadsheet to keep track of the dates you've booked so far. It could be a simple calendar, or it could be similar to the example in the download pack.

Download the Examples Pack from my website by scanning the below QR code:

Password: examplespack1

Types of Buyers/Organisations

We'll now learn about the main types of 'buyer' you're likely to be dealing with regularly: venue promoters, concert promoters, and festival bookers.

Venues

I won't go into detail listing the myriad of different types of venues available to perform in, as you'll most likely know the differences between performing arts centres, house concerts and club gigs for example. You should know though, that the principles are generally the same across them all.

Most professional venues book many acts 'in-house' (they put on the shows and take the financial risk) whilst at the same time hiring their spaces out to external organisers—concert promoters.

Their resulting programme will often be a mix of shows booked, promoted, and underwritten by the venue, and those on an 'external hire' where a concert promoter has paid them to hire the space.

In the case of the external hire, the venue still has an interest in the show doing well (at the very least for their bar sales), but not overall responsibility to fill the room and pay artists, which lies with the hiree, or concert promoter.

Some venues only do one or the other; either booking in-house or hiring out to external event organisers (they don't 'buy in' shows). As a rule, most venues do both and you'll either be contacting the venue directly (common in the early stages of a band's career), or contacting a promoter first, who will then liaise with the venue, make the booking, and take the financial risk of putting on the show.

Concert Promoters

Known as presenters in North America, these are hugely important for the 'bigger picture' of your touring career. Taking full responsibility of booking and delivering the show, a promoter makes their living by ensuring rooms are full and money is made, for both the artists, and themselves.

In the UK, there are many promoters that are not out to make money from shows; they might run gigs in houses, (house concerts) the back rooms of pubs, community events in village halls, or they might simply be enthusiasts/supporters of the artists and are just happy to be involved.

It is likely your tours will comprise of some shows from these 'hobby' organisers to start with, but as your profile increases, so too will the involvement of more professional, full-time concert promoters, especially if you do get picked up by a booking agent.

Like agents, concert promoters can be big, small, independent, or part of a conglomerate, but they all ultimately help grow and shape the careers of the artists they present.

So why should you enlist the help of a promoter, rather than book direct with the venue?

There is no one-size-fits-all approach as such, however some points to consider are:

- Venues are often standalone, whereas a promoter can use a myriad of different venues.
- A promoter could start working with an artist in the early days in small venues, and as the relationship develops, become a solid part of the artist's team, taking them to the next level venue at each step and 'growing' the artist.

- It is hugely beneficial having an extra level of promotion for a gig. Sure, the venue might have a whole marketing department, list the show on their website, include in their brochure if they have one, send to their email list and shout about it on social media, but using a promoter, you're getting that twice. The promoter may well also have their own audience, a large mailing list, take out regular adverts in all the right outlets, and use multiple ticketing sales agents (thus increasing reach further). They also have a great incentive to make your show sell as well as possible —their payday.

- Promoters often have their own 'identity' and 'associations'. They might present all the hippest music in town, use only the coolest venues, be known for niches like Glam Rock or Cajun, or be perceived as tastemakers; any of which could make them a promoter that an artist wants to be associated with.

- Promoters are a bit like agents, record labels, and festival organisers; they are big networkers and are well connected in the wider industry. Furthermore, if a festival sees a promoter has started working with a band, the band might be more likely to get a booking at that festival; either because of the association, or simply because the festival organiser and promoter are friends.

- Promoters often run, or are involved in running festivals, thereby increasing your likelihood of getting a booking at said festival.

- Some promoters specialise regionally (regional promoters) and might be known as the 'go-to' people in a certain part of the country. Some promoters put shows on across the country, often 'buying' several dates, or even the entire tour (national promoters). The latter tend to be the big players, and unless artists are selling around 300 tickets per gig across the country, a national promoter is unlikely to want to get involved in any area they deem risky (usually anywhere outside of the capital/biggest market).

- Many promoters actually own and/or operate their own venues.

So how can I get a promoter to put on my shows?

For the promoter, it's about commercial viability, and being one step ahead in knowing which artists might become so. Like agents, they are always looking for new artists to get involved with.

Firstly, it's about the fit; looking at which promoters are best suited to your music, and thinking about what you're trying to achieve from any association. Secondly, it's a case of pitching to them and being enough of an attractive prospect that they'll want to do a show for you.

Festivals - Promoters/Bookers

Festivals are of course hugely important for artists of all levels to be playing. They are a quick way to get in front of a new audience, provide a platform for selling a lot of merchandise, and create good leverage for getting other bookings. Festivals are in themselves influential, and their bookers are some of the most influential people in the music industry.

The bigger the festival, the bigger the 'celebrity' the booker is in the industry. Known for their exquisite tastes and ahead-of-the-curve bookings, everyone wants to be in a room with them.

The booker might be the actual main organiser of the festival or be an individual working as part of a larger festival team.

It's common to see bookers of big festivals also chairing boards of other industry bodies, chatting on panel sessions at conferences, and generally being some of the busiest people in the business; travelling regularly and attending gigs most nights of the week (invite them!).

The best tactic with festivals is to pitch to them early and get a long conversation going as the months go by. The booking period for most summer festivals in the UK, for instance, usually runs from September – February. Most will have booked their biggest acts by the new year (through agents!) and will be working their way down the bill from there.

An even better tactic would be to try to meet them in person. As we've already discussed, think about attending an industry conference (did you apply?) where they'll most likely be hanging around with many similar high-profile bookers.

At these events, most are happy to meet (with an advance request) and though they are bombarded with pitches, remember it is their job to be, so get in there!

Be tenacious about getting on the radars of bookers; because of the friends they have and the company they keep (other bookers), the results of your efforts will be compounded as your name is mentioned amongst them.

Key Takeaways from Chapter 5:

- The music industry is a great example of it not being 'what you know, but who you know'. Get yourself out and about.

- Even though your approaches might be coming from the band directly, make it look as professional as possible.

- Get together an organised system so you can find your contacts, keep track of who you've pitched to (and when), and maintain your calendar.

- Venues book artists directly, but promoters also book artists in venues. There are many reasons artists might book with a promoter rather than directly with the venue.

- Get on the radars of, and build up rapports with festival bookers to get on the festivals.

Chapter 6: Strategy and Booking

It's nearly time to get started pitching for shows and festivals, and getting those bookings in, but first, a lesson on strategy.

Strategy

In this section, I will try to give you an insight into how an agent thinks, based on some of the common scenarios and predicaments we encounter on a regular basis.

Describing the 'thinking' element of an agent's role is tricky to explain over the medium of a book, but I feel it is important to try to, and with the examples I outline in this section, hopefully you'll begin to understand more about the thought process and decision-making that goes into them.

Strategy Example 1: Touring Around an Album Release.
Do you have a plan? To maximise your potential, you should have a long-term plan, with defined goals and actionable steps you can take to realise them. Don't just tour for the sake of touring or release a record because you feel like you should. Start with a 'why?'

An artist's career tends to move in cycles, and I often think of touring (and perceived 'profile') visualised as a wave; you build up and build up until the crest, then roll off again until the next one comes around. For most artists, the 'crest' is the period of time around the release of a new record (when interest and exposure are at their peak), and strategically speaking, this will be the best time for them to go out on the road.

Decisions such as album release schedules are usually made by the artist/management in consultation with the agent—touring is now such an integral part of a campaign, that it makes sense to work out a strategy together as to maximise the benefits of each.

The album might be due to come out either in spring or winter. Or maybe you've not decided yet. Let's look at some potential scenarios, breaking the year up into four quarters (Q).

Album-release and Tour in Spring:

Q1
Q2 – album release followed by tour
Q3
Q4

This model is common, but it means working backwards so that by Q3 of the previous year, you have everything lined up, including the tour mostly booked, so it can be announced late in Q4 of that year, and then announced again after Christmas in your 'focus' year. Q1 could include a single release to get the anticipation building:

Q3 (of previous year) – tour booked
Q4 – new album announced, tour announced
Q1 (of focus year) – first single, album reminder, tour reminder
Q2 – album release followed by tour*
Q3
Q4

*It's best to wait around six weeks after the album is released before starting the tour. This gives everyone the best chance to have fully noticed its release, and to have listened to it. It also gives time for a PR campaign to have properly started and hopefully delivering results by the time the tour starts.

You could (and should) release something later in the year to maintain the momentum and extract as much value from the release 'cycle' as you can:

Q3 (of previous year) – tour booked
Q4 – new album announced, tour announced
Q1 (of focus year) – first single, album reminder, tour reminder
Q2 – album release followed by tour
Q3
Q4 – second single release

You could also (and again, should) build in the summer festivals, which offer a great platform to sell records:

Q3 (of previous year) – tour booked
Q4 – new album announced, tour announced
Q1 (of focus year) – first single, album reminder, tour reminder
Q2 – album release followed by tour, into summer festivals
Q3 – summer festivals
Q4 – second single release

Or wait, have we missed an opportunity? Playing in front of so many people at the summer festivals perhaps seems like a waste in that any potential new fans will have missed out on the tour dates this time around. Maybe it would be a good idea to build in some dates at the back end of the year to capitalise on these:

Q3 (of previous year) – tour booked
Q4 – new album announced, tour announced
Q1 (of focus year) – first single, album reminder, tour reminder
Q2 – album release followed by tour, into summer festivals
Q3 – summer festivals
Q4 – second single release + tour of secondary markets*

*A secondary market tour is a great 'second shot' at going back out on the road, giving you the opportunity to include some of the perhaps less obvious towns/cities you missed first time around. It might also offer the venues that couldn't be persuaded to take a chance on you initially, the opportunity to reconsider (after seeing the exposure you're getting).

That's one scenario, but let's look now at releasing later in the year.

Album-release and Tour in Winter:

Releasing the album and touring in winter is another popular model.

You'll notice we don't mention summer. Summer (in the UK, for example) is a difficult time to tour as people are mostly on holiday, spending their money on music festivals, or just enjoying barbeques at home.

The most popular touring months (again from a UK point of view) are March, April, May, October, and November. Coincidentally, these are also the most popular months to release a new record. It can get crowded, and again, the early planners will reap better rewards.

Let's consider an album release in November:

Q1
Q2 – tour announcement
Q3 –
Q4 – album release followed by tour

We essentially have the entire year to 'set up', which makes this a very popular model.

The tour would need to be booked and announced by Q2 to allow time to set up and sell tickets (selling tickets over summer is notoriously slow, so it's best to get the shows on sale before May).

A single could be released (or 'dropped', as the cool kids say) in spring with the announcement, and also another in late summer just before the record is released:

Q1
Q2 – tour announcement + first single release
Q3 –
Q4 – second single, then album release, then tour

Summer festivals could help to sell the single, build up excitement and demand for the album, and sell tickets for the tour (all those new fans will want to see you again, right?) thus:

Q1
Q2 – tour announcement + first single release, into summer festivals
Q3 – summer festivals
Q4 – second single, then album release, then tour

Taking this further, we could then see Christmas through, and 'drop' a third single in the new year (nicely keeping the momentum ticking over during the holiday season) and provide prospective festivals (in year two) with an even better reason (and urgency) to book you.

In addition, you could also do a secondary markets tour in Q2:

(It's also worth noting that in this model, **you'll be pitching for the festivals at the exact time your profile/cycle will be reaching its 'crest'** as your record comes out—which of course gives you an excellent advantage.)

Q1
Q2 – tour announcement + first single release, into summer festivals
Q3 – summer festivals
Q4 – second single, then album release, then tour. Pitch for festivals.
Q1 (of year two) – third single release

Q2 – secondary markets tour/summer festivals
Q3 – summer festivals

Comparing these models, I'd be leaning towards the release in winter, as it gives you a story/leverage to get summer festivals, to then use the summer festivals to help sell tickets for the main tour (and sell the record), whilst remaining a 'fresh' (i.e. having had a recent release, and still in the public eye) and attractive prospect for the festivals you didn't manage to secure first time around.

My take? As you can see, it's all about structuring the timing and release plan so you're leveraging the maximum you can from your efforts; from picking the best times of the year to tour, to getting the summer festivals that can seriously help you raise your game. I'm also increasingly noticing (and liking) more and more artists putting out a series of releases prior to the album being released; perhaps five or six singles. For a long time, this has been a common model in the Hip-Hop genre, which is often one step ahead of most other genres in terms of innovation. As soon as the album is out, that's the end of your campaign, and in this world, the longer that campaign lasts, the longer you'll remain interesting. But I'm just the agent—what do I know?

Strategy Example 2: Thoughts on Choosing Venue Sizes.

As an agent, I'm generally trying to place my artists into the smallest possible venues.

Now that sounds a bit odd on first inspection I agree, but bear with me while I explain.

The best result an artist can hope to achieve from a show is that it reaches sell-out. It's at this point their maximum earning potential is realised (tickets and merchandise), the promoter is in good spirits and has made money, and the audience has had a great time knowing they're part of a select few who are witnessing something special happening right in front of them—and being very aware that some people have missed out.

The crucial thing here is exactly that: people have missed out.

A sold-out show creates many more (also perhaps intangible) benefits than first meets the eye. Ok, the artist has made a good amount of money, and yes, the promoter is delighted and definitely wants to book you again (maybe in a different venue with an increase in capacity next time!), but the single most important benefit in terms of an artist's career, is that people have missed out.

Nothing creates urgency like a sold-out show. Everyone wants a piece of something they can't get, and the people who didn't bother buying a ticket in advance *("I'm sure we can just rock up on the night, they're not that well known")* will be first in line next time, having had a stark realisation of just how well you are in fact doing. Suddenly their favourite band has become popular, and the wave of new fans has stopped them getting into the gig.

It's like compounded interest. They tell their friends to get in early next time, who, in turn, tell *their* friends *"it will sell out, so get your ticket in advance"*, then they'll tell their friends how you're *"going to be huge"* and so on.

Shouting on your social media that a show is sold-out is another great thing. Anyone who previously might not have given you the time of day will now be taking notice.

If you get the word out properly, you may also start to notice an increase in people wanting a piece of you professionally. The promoter who didn't reply last time will now be messaging you asking if you're keen on doing another show soon (this time, with them), and the festival booker who previously ignored you might now be replying to your emails after you gently reminded them that your last show sold out in advance. It doesn't matter if it had a capacity of fifty or five hundred, a sold-out show is a sold-out show.

So, as an agent, I'm generally trying to put my artists in the smallest possible venues.

Don't get me wrong, I'm also trying to always increase the capacity and ticket price gradually over time, but it's a delicate balancing act; one false move and the momentum is lost.

Ever wonder why you sometimes see 'big' names doing smaller-than-expected gigs? Maybe their last album didn't receive as much traction as they'd hoped, and they found themselves down a hole with little interest. As soon as they announce a small show, it sells out, and their interest is on the up again.

The oldest trick in the book is when agents consistently place their artists into 'too small' venues (known as an 'underplay'). You let the demand rocket, before taking them away for a while (writing, or touring in a different country perhaps) and on their return, have them playing arenas. How on earth did that happen? A bit of clever strategy and psychology, with of course a bit of calculated risk sprinkled on top for good measure.

My take? If you play small, you actually play big. Even if you might have sold more tickets than you would have done in a smaller space, there is nothing worse than playing to a half-empty room—with all due respect, as I imagine you well know.

Strategy Example 3: Thoughts on Strategic Goodwill to Get Results.

The agent of band *The Big Old* really thinks they should be playing at *Park Festival* next year, which is promoted/organised by top promoter *Tide Presents*.

The Big Old has a new record out later in the year and their agent is about to start booking the tour. They have lots of interest already.

It would make sense for the agent to pitch for a show (and start building a relationship) with *Tide Presents*, in the hope that they might take the show, and subsequently consider them for the festival once they see how well it did.

Sadly, the band isn't booked for the show (and now has the involvement of another promoter), but the conversation is maintained, and is instead offered a slot at a different festival *Tide Presents* runs later in the year, which is accepted. *The Big Old* plays the festival and seriously impresses the team at *Tide Presents.*

After playing the festival, the agent keeps the conversation going and pitches again for a concert show, and this time, having already worked with the band, *Tide Presents* offers to promote a few shows on the tour.

These shows do well, and a long-term relationship is built, facilitated by the agent, and cemented by the band meeting the promoter at the shows and going out for drinks with the whole team afterwards.

Next time, *Tide Presents* not only books further shows for the band in other markets, but also puts them forward for a couple of other festivals they aren't even involved with, but have strong influence over. By doing these festivals, it means they can (all) move up to the next level. They are now ready to play *Park Festival*, and the offer is made.

The agent now only goes to *Tide Presents* for shows in the strongest markets of the country; with a shared interest, both parties work closely and continue to grow the band **together**.

My take? Think about who you work with, what else they might be involved with, and how you could benefit from building a relationship long term with them.

Strategy Example 4: Career-Building Shows vs Money-Making Shows.

We know an agent gets paid from taking a cut of the artist's fee. Any good agent however won't always go for the best-paid gig, but the best opportunity for their artist. It's a balancing act of ensuring you are getting the best possible fees on one hand, but at the same time helping you actually build your career by going after the right kind of shows—even if it means taking a lower offer. In the next chapter we'll be looking into actual offers and deal structures, and this will further reinforce the notion that a band's worth equates simply to their draw—i.e. how many tickets they are able to sell.

But for now, let me try to explain in the most basic terms with a fairly common example:

The Pigs Ear Inn and The Lexington are both pub venues in London.

The Pigs Ear Inn runs regular open mic nights, has a quiz on Thursdays, karaoke on a Friday, and live music on Saturday nights. Bands however must be playing well-known cover songs for people to dance to. Their offer is an attractive £800.

The Lexington has a dedicated 'live room', and a vast array of promoters regularly hire the room out. It's well known for being cool, and lots of bands play there on their way up.

With an attractive ticket price, the offer for a show here is £200 vs 80% box office split. Even if you sell out here, you're only likely to make around £400.

Hopefully, it's quite obvious which would be the better show to take here (The Lexington). Although the offer for the show at the Lexington is low in comparison, it will be most likely with a promoter, thus giving the artist an association, exposure, and platform on which to build. There is nothing cool or constructive in playing other people's songs to inebriated dancers in our context…

Another (slightly more nuanced) example would be the following scenario of two potential show offers in Bristol:

The first offer is from St Greenods Village Hall; a community hall on the outskirts of town which regularly puts on original music nights. They've booked various bands in a similar style to yours, and even some musicians you know have played there. They hope to sell 150 tickets and will offer you £1000 to play for them. Sounds like a good deal.

The second offer is from the Louisiana in Bristol; a small (but legendary) venue in the city centre, and like the above Lexington example, is a 'hire only' venue and some of the biggest concert promoters in the country start their relationships with their smaller artists in its c100 capacity space.

The offer here on the table is from one of these such promoters, but is a somewhat risky 75% of the box office income. No guaranteed fee.

From an agent's point of view, a band is **always better playing in venues on the 'circuit' that their audience is likely to be already familiar with.**

Although the show at the community hall would likely be a good gig (and a good payday), it just doesn't carry the same 'look' or weight as a show at the Louisiana would. Their audience screams of a 'built in' crowd of local supporters, which on one hand is good (new fans?) but on the other, they're probably not going to travel to your next gig in the city centre, and are perhaps there more in support of their community, and for something to do on a Saturday night, than to have actually come to see you per se. Please forgive the generalisations here.

Sadly, this type of show is just not 'cool' and in most cases, won't help towards the upward progression of the band. Remember, as agents, we are always trying to take the most direct and efficient route upwards, make the best associations, and get the best opportunities for our clients.

Trying to get your band booked at a major festival and boasting that they've just sold out St Greenods Village Hall (vs selling out a show at the Louisiana) really gives the promoter of the festival an insight into what kind of band you are, and crucially, what stage in your career you are at. Why would you not be playing city-centre Bristol (where your target market and biggest potential audience lies) if you were on the up?

My take? Make things easy for yourself, and for your audience. Play the venues on the circuit that people have heard of, and you are, by default, choosing the most direct route to the top. Though sometimes tempting when financial offers are good elsewhere, anything else will be a distraction and dilution of your brand. Save these shows for an 'off' year; they will always be there. In this example, selling out the Louisiana means you have the proof of your draw and thus somewhere to go to next; somewhere bigger. Selling out St Greenods Village Hall means you'd then still have to do a 'real' hard-ticket show at the Louisiana (and sell it out) to get to the same position and be able to progress. A good agent is always thinking about the next step.

Strategy Example 5: Support Tours

Tour support slots are something agents are always pitching their artists for because they are so good for an artist's exposure and are beneficial even for established artists.

An opening slot on a tour with a bigger name offers a great opportunity for the building artist; playing in front of a ready-made audience, jumping on the back of all the publicity and marketing that has gone into promoting the tour, and of course the chance to gain potentially hundreds of new fans from not only the shows, but also the association with the bigger artist. It's no wonder competition is rife to secure them.

I'm often asked how artists can go about getting a support tour. In truth, it's a team effort, and from experience, often an initial artist-artist relationship is a key, if not instigating factor.

The headline band is much more likely to want to share their tour with an artist they're already friendly with (rather than a seemingly random opener the record label or agent has packaged them with) and the final say in most cases will come down to the headline artist in question.

I suggest to my artists to cultivate these artist-artist relationships and plant the seeds with others they can think of that they might have even a vague connection to.

It's then a case of me (the agent) speaking with the headline artist's agent (and/or manager), and the manager of my artist speaking to the manager of the headline artist. Often, it's a combination of agent-agent, agent-manager, manager-manager, manager-artist, manager-record label, artist-artist, etc. discussions. Sometimes everything comes together, and the tour happens, sometimes it doesn't.

It is still the case that 'buy-ons' exist, where smaller artists pay the headline band to be the support act. This isn't that common and not a model I'm fond of.

My take? Think about other artists you know, or could get to know. Again, if you don't ask, you don't get. Keep knocking on doors.

Strategy Example 6: Frequency of Shows/Limiting How Much You Perform

You can die of exposure, as they say.

Artists often forget that the music industry is a market, and the business will, whether we like it or not, operate like one.

So yes, supply and demand. Too much supply and the demand plummets. Too much demand? Well, that's slightly better, but even then, it's about acting at the right time to capitalise on it.

I often see artists simply gigging too much, and one of my first pieces of advice is usually to do less, especially in your hometown. People have to really value it when you do play, and not come to expect or be able to set their watches by your live plans. It comes back to making everything an occasion; an event they just can't miss. There is nothing like a sense of urgency, intrigue or surprise to motivate fans.

To give an example in UK terms, I'd suggest playing London perhaps only twice a year to maintain upward growth. Artists should do fewer shows but ones of bigger stature. You are better to be able to guarantee selling out two shows, than half-filling three.

On a different, but similar point, I also frequently see bands playing for too long at their shows. I personally feel a tight set of seventy-five mins (+ encore) is about right if there is one support act. If there are two support acts (try to avoid!), it should be more like sixty-five minutes. Anything over this risks challenging your audience's attention span, and as an audience member, as soon as you've looked at your watch, you know the artist has lost you. You always want to leave your audience wanting more; whether that's because you've not played their city for a while (always be due a visit somewhere!) or you've played the perfect set length at your gig. Keep them hungry.

My take? Limit how much of 'live' you your audience can get. Don't over-saturate your markets (or your set lengths). Less is often more.

Summary

I hope the above examples give you an insight into how an agent thinks, how they might build a plan with an artist, and reinforce how relationships affect everything. I've said this before, but networks really are the cogs of the music industry machinery.

I'd recommend taking some time to consider the above scenarios carefully. Every artist is different and there are always other ways of doing things. Think how you've approached things in the past, and what your strategies going forward might look like.

It's time to start booking.

Booking

Before we start, I'm sure you've gathered by now that being an agent is very much a sales job. Not everyone will want to buy what you are selling, and it's therefore important to keep in mind that you're dealing with human beings at the other end of your communications. We all know what and who we like, and we can at times be fickle, socially political, and have a bias towards what (and who) we already know. Being respectful and easy to deal with will help you tremendously.

To begin, my advice would be to outline a three-week period within your chosen touring timeframe, with the aim of getting a tight, concise run of dates within this, based on the best venue availabilities you can get.

Ensure you have a target list (hopefully you will have this already from the previous chapter), and that whenever you are pitching, you're writing to the correct person. This could be the promoter, the venue booker or festival organiser. If I'm unsure, I'll often make a quick generic call to the venue (trying *not* to speak with the booker, but someone else who works there) asking for clarification that XXXX (get a name, even if you're sure it's old!) is indeed still the booker. If not, they will usually correct you and be happy to share the new contact details. If you do just get a name, or are fobbed off with a generic info@ address, you will most likely be able to find their email address online with some clever search engine-eering, and perhaps a bit of guesswork.

Be certain you have their full name, can spell it correctly (!), and have their correct email address. Hopefully, again with some clever Google-ing, you have also managed to find a contact number for them.

Ensure you keep your spreadsheet updated of your progress; it can be hugely embarrassing chasing someone for an answer who has already said 'no'. As a reminder, your data should detail at minimum the event/venue name, the booker's name, email address and telephone number, and allow you to enter the date you pitched, the date you nudged, the date the last contact was made, and the result (yes/no/no response).

It's important to remember these bookers are busy people. Often it can come down to a case of whoever shouts the loudest gets the response but remember it's a fine line between reminding someone how keen you are, to seriously annoying them and getting yourself blacklisted.

So, what should the perfect pitch look like?

My Top Tips to Ensure You Stand Out in a Booker's Inbox:

- Always personalise the email with the name of who you're writing to.

- Introduce yourself, what you are pitching for, and the act you're pitching.

- Talk about recent news, notable performances to date, and plans going forwards. Having a plan looks good. If you have any history of touring, mention it.

- Include a couple of great pictures (one studio and one live).

- Ensure your website and social media is up to date. The booker will probably be checking on here to see a) how many followers you have engaging with you (and thus judging your ability to motivate/draw your fans) and b) that you'll be doing your bit to push the gig from your end if you get a date booked in.

- Include a link to two of your best YouTube videos; one live (ideally at a high-profile event and professionally filmed) and a studio video. The sound on both should be good.

- Include a couple of good quotes from reputable sources if you have them. A bland quote from a big-name or known press outlet is better than a great quote from someone the booker has never heard of.

- Include a link to some online music; ideally an album stream link. A 'private' link always looks good and feels special, especially if it's pre-release.

- Keep it short, ideally no longer than three good paragraphs. Good copy shouldn't be a life story, but a punchy description of what you actually do. Sell the benefits: "*we always get people on their feet*" or, "*we can easily sell three tickets in this city*" etc.

- Try to briefly explain what you'll do at your end to help sell the show and how you'll promote it to your fans.

- Your email pitch should be written in your 'voice', but once you've signed it off with 'Please find more detailed information below', you can paste in your usual bio/blurb.

- Keep the tone friendly, edging on persuasive.

- Don't mention any fees/tickets/other expectations in the first pitch.

- Include your contact phone number in your email signature.

OK, let's press send.

It's now a waiting game. Check to see what they're up to on social media during this time. Give them a 'Like' or a retweet perhaps?

If you hear nothing back, I'd recommend waiting fourteen days and giving them a nudge. I find something like the following works well:

Hi _____—I wondered if you may have had a chance to look at the below?

I would love to discuss with you.

thanks,

_____

(with the original email you sent pasted in below)

Remember to make a note in your file of when the email was sent, and when the follow-up was sent.

If you haven't heard anything after your follow-up, you could try calling them. This can be scary at first until you get used to it, but remember these people are bookers. That's what they do. For many of them, this will be their job. If you don't call them, someone else will.

You could miss out the follow-up email and go straight to the call after the first email, but it's important to find a balance and not be too pushy.

If you can have a chat with the person on the phone, it gives you a chance to build some rapport, ask if 'they've had a chance to check out your email yet?' and allow them to be on their way without commitment, saying you'll drop them a line in a week or so. Don't push for an answer there and then, just make it obvious that you're not afraid to call them up and badger them (by doing just that).

Usually you'll be able to get a reply and subsequent email conversation going from then on.

From this point, rather than constantly nagging, a good tip would be to drip-feed them some exciting news updates every ten days or so, and remind them how 'keen you are to be considered'.

Ensure you're still engaging with them **subtly** from time to time on social media. One of the great things about social media is being able to feel as though you're in the next room to someone, just so they catch sight of you!

If the answer is a 'no', that shouldn't be the end of your journey by any means. Thank them for their time and think about what it is they're looking for. At least you have a conversation going with them now, and you can try pitching again another time for a future date.

Being persistent is the key; pitching, following up, and playing the long game. It is also very much a numbers game. The more pitches you send, of course, the higher chance you have of success.

This industry is small, and you'll likely run into the same people time and time again, for the same (and different) events. Be remembered for being nice. People want to work with people they like, and no matter how frustrating it can be at times, keep your cool, be polite, and don't be afraid to call them up every now and again to update them with what's been happening in your world, gently reminding them that you're still keen to chat about a date/slot'.

Routing

You may be familiar with the term 'routing', which describes how each date follows on from another, or how the run of dates 'flows' geographically. In the fields of computer science and operations, it is a common algorithmic riddle known as the Travelling Salesman Problem; the challenge of finding the shortest and most efficient (in terms of time and fuel) route between a given list of specific destinations.

The most common and sensible format starts and finishes the tour in your home area, taking in every venue on the tour in a circular return trip. To achieve this, it's usually a case of 'pencilling' a couple of dates at each venue whilst the tour takes shape, before confirming the best one at each. If a date you want is already pencilled, many venues operate a 'challenge' system, where you can give the other date-holder twenty-four hours to confirm or release the date–but understand that means it can happen to you also!

Though a good agent prides themselves on how well routed their tours are, it's rarely possible to get an absolutely flawless routing. I once sent a band from Edinburgh, Scotland to Brighton on the South coast of England on consecutive days! They had to fly. It was however their decision, and it was either that, or no (great, and well-paid) gig in Brighton.

One of the things I've learnt over the years is that although the routing is important, and bad routing can make or break a tour financially, the shows are actually what is important. If the show is right (in terms of opportunity, profile, or financially) and the band should be doing it, even if it means a nonsensical U-turn in routing because of the limited availability the venue has, they should do it, and any serious band will understand that.

I often remind my artists that no opportunity is comparable, and every deal, promoter, circumstance and market is different. For some shows they will be overpaid, and for some shows they'll be underpaid–according to their expectations, anyway. What matters is that it all balances up in the end in terms of profit or profile.

My Expert Booking Tips:

- Start booking as early as you can (within reason!) to get the best pick of the dates, and thus the best routing. Ten months in advance is ideal.

- In UK terms, Wednesdays and Thursdays are the best nights to play London as industry/press etc. are difficult to get out on weekends! This may be the same for other countries' main 'music' cities.

- Give yourself a Monday (or a couple of Mondays) off. These are usually the hardest nights to get, and do, unless there is an established event or concert series that runs on this night.

- Try to avoid touring around public holidays; in experience, touring around these dates often results in lower ticket sales.

- If accommodation is offered as part of the deal, check what it means. It could be a hotel in addition to a straight fee, or it could be a 'show cost' to be covered before any overage (backend percentage break bonus) is made—in which case, you might be paying for it anyway if it's a busy night. Or it could be private 'homestay' with the organiser or a friend of the venue, which is common. Ask the question so there are no surprises. Communication is a key skill in agent-land, and covering your back is another. A good agent avoids their artists being surprised!

- Always ask promoters to keep you in the loop about any support slots they might have available that they think you could be a good fit for. Remind them that you're 'in this for the long game' and want to invest in your career. A simple act like this might just land you some nice support slots that could be more worthwhile than your own headline show and/or could be done to set up a later headline show.

- Remember that as much as you're out to get deals, you should be out to form relationships with the bookers too. Again, be nice.

Key Takeaways from Chapter 6:

- Think about strategy. What is the reason to tour? Will there be a release?

- Think about the best time to tour.

- Always play venues that are on the small side. Sell out and you've always got somewhere to progress to.

- Start your booking process ideally ten months in advance.

- Keep your spreadsheet up to date so you know when the last time you contacted someone was.

- Keep your pitch brief but include all the essentials. Be persuasive yet friendly.

- Don't take getting no response for a 'no'.

- A call will always yield better results and is a quicker route to rapport. Get comfortable with it.

- You will face setbacks and rejection, but understand this is a normal part of this area of the industry. Develop a thick skin and keep going.

- Don't forget the value of support slots.

- Start booking early to get the best routing. Hold a couple of dates at each venue until the tour takes shape and you can choose the best option at each.

- Don't adopt a 'catch-all' model to fees. Every show is different, and good opportunities rarely fit into 'usual' fee expectations.

- Remember you should be aiming to form long-term relationships with the bookers you are pitching to.

Things to Do Now 2:

Task 5:

Spend some time thinking about what your run of dates might look like and jot down some ideas, including a rough time frame. Will there be a record release? If so, will it be an album? Will there be a single? Or several singles? When might you want to tour?

Task 6:

It's now time to start work pitching for the venues that are on your hitlist. Start drafting, roughly planning the routing and the pitch using the tips you've picked up from the previous chapter. Check it, and check it again before pressing send. In the next chapter you'll learn about deals and fees so don't 'talk money' until reading on.

Task 7

Create a list of potential artists you could approach about a support tour. Do your research, think ahead and think creatively. See if they have any tours planned and mention this in the email. If they don't, it's still worth contacting them again for a future tour. Remember to send emails to the band, and to any management, agent, and record label/publishing contacts they have listed on their websites. You will probably be bounced ultimately to the same people you've written to already by writing to these, but there is no harm in doing so; it's certainly a good way to get on their radars and show them how hard-working you are!

Chapter 7: Deals and Negotiation

You hopefully now have some pencilled dates, and some early discussions are happening around the financials of your proposed shows.

A good booking agent should be a highly skilled negotiator; firm but fair.

Though you'll want to get as much money as you can for your shows, it's important to be realistic about what fee you believe you should be able to command, and to balance the risk between yourself (the artist) and the promoter. Both parties should feel good about the deal.

Having two 'customers' to keep happy can be one of the most challenging aspects of being an agent; of course I work for (and get my fee from) the artists, but at the same time I'm conscious that I will be regularly seeking subsequent bookings from the same promoters, venues, and festivals for other artists on my roster.

The principles of a fair deal are the same no matter where you are in the world, and the only thing that really changes is the saleability or 'worth' and demand of the product (artist) in question, and how well you negotiate.

If you have been consistently touring for a while, have built up a fan base and have a 'draw' (you 'draw' people to come and see you), you are likely to be 'worth' much more (in terms of commercial viability i.e. ticket sales) to a promoter/venue/festival than you would be if it were your first time playing in a specified town, for example.

You should negotiate the best fees you can, while remembering you are in it for the long game. Scaring promoters off with a naively pitched exorbitant fee (or likewise getting the fee and bankrupting the promoter!) will set you back, if not destroy, your chances with that particular buyer.

Our ultimate goal is to get what I call your 'demand ratio' to flip, so that rather than you having to be always the one pitching/following up/ begging for shows, the phone doesn't stop ringing with people wanting to book *you*, instantly giving you the upper hand in negotiations.

Many of the established agents representing some of the biggest names habitually don't quote fees but simply invite offers. This is both a test of a promoters' experience and nerve, and grotesque display of the agents' gall; a tactic to attain the highest fee possible, knowing they have the upper hand: the buyers are in most cases coming to them. A proverbial game of cat-and-mouse quickly follows, and if the promoter's offer is too low, they'll be shot down. Too high, and they'll have most likely paid over the odds.

As I've stated already, it all comes down to the market. Unlike a product in plentiful supply, a product in demand can, and will command a higher price. Don't be seen to be chronically 'available', even if your diary is clear!

Typical Fees/Deal Structures

Here we'll examine some of the types of deals you're likely to come across, with basic examples to illustrate how they work.

Straight guaranteed fee deal (common)

Example Offer: guaranteed fee of £500.

Venue Capacity   100
Ticket Price   £10
Show Costs*   £100

'Potential' (capacity x ticket price – show costs) = £900

Here the artist receives the guaranteed fee no matter how many tickets have been sold.

If only 20 tickets are sold (value £200), the artist receives the £500 guarantee.

If all 100 tickets are sold (value £1000), artist still only receives £500.

You'll see from the straight guaranteed fee, it's good for the artist if they're unsure of their draw, but also bad for them if the show does very well, as they won't earn any extra income.

Guaranteed fee versus split of the door deal (common)

Offer example: guaranteed fee of £500 vs 80% split after venue costs.

Venue Capacity   100
Ticket Price   £10
Show Costs*   £100

'Potential' (capacity x ticket price - show costs) = £900

If only 20 tickets are sold (value £200), artist receives £500 guarantee. If all 100 tickets are sold (value £1000), artist receives £720 (80% of sales less costs).

The guarantee vs % deal is perhaps the most common you'll encounter. It's a good model as it allows the artist to earn more if it's a busy night, whilst not exposing the promoter to a big initial fee. It balances risk on both sides.

Guaranteed fee plus split of the door deal (less common)

Offer example: guarantee of £500 plus 70% split after venue costs.

Venue Capacity   100
Ticket Price   £10
Show Costs*   £100+£500 band guaranteed fee = £600

'Potential' (capacity x ticket price - show costs) = £400

If only 20 tickets are sold (value £200), artist receives £500 guarantee. If all 100 tickets are sold (value £1000), artist receives £780 (£500+70% of gross sales less costs).

The guarantee + % deal is less common but you're likely to still see it from time to time. It is a good deal for the artist, but not as much for the promoter, as it significantly diminishes their potential profit.

Door split deal (common) - also known as **80/20** deal (or 70/30 etc.)

Offer example: 90% of box office income after show costs

Venue Capacity   100
Ticket Price   £10
Show Costs*   £100

'Potential' (capacity x ticket price − show costs) = £900

If only 20 tickets are sold (value £200), artist receives £90

If all 100 tickets are sold (value £1000), artist receives £810

The door split deal is a risky option for artists; if it doesn't sell well, their fee could be very small, or even zero. It's very low-risk for the promoter and is a common scenario if the artist wants the gig but the promoter isn't convinced on how it will sell. It's also common if the artist is certain about their draw as show costs will often be reduced (and possibly shared with the promoter) if there isn't a guaranteed fee to risk on top.

First Call deal (less common)

Offer example: First call to artist of £500, followed by second call to venue of £300, thereafter 70% of remains to artist.

Venue Capacity   100
Ticket Price   £10

'Potential' (capacity x ticket price) = £1000

In this deal, there is no guaranteed fee, but the artist keeps all ticket income money up to £500. The promoters' show costs are absorbed into their portion of the 'call'.

If only 20 tickets are sold (value £200), artist receives £200
If all 100 tickets are sold (value £1000), artist receives £640 (£500 + 70% of the £200 left after the second call 'remains'.

The First Call deal isn't that common, but is another model sometimes used to balance the risk across both parties.

Reflecting on the above, there aren't really any secrets here; it's about looking at what a fair deal is to you, and only you can decide that.

Throughout the negotiation and offer process, an agent will discuss carefully with the promoter about ticket pricing, and often take the promoter's experience of his/her audience into consideration. It does however make sense to keep ticket prices roughly similar across a tour, as to not annoy fans who might find they have to pay more in some areas than in others.

It's also important that as a band progresses, the ticket price for their shows increases too, allowing them to maintain their worth in the market and generate more revenue per show. An artist's growth is facilitated by the consistent increase in venue capacity and ticket price, but if these increase too quickly, they will come unstuck by market forces and have to step backwards.

*A quick note about show costs. These are the costs that the promoter will have to put up and risk to organise the show. It's very normal for these costs to be recouped before the artist makes any extra fee ('overage', as it's called) on a percentage/backend deal.

Show costs vary hugely, and in most cases will be broken down into categories such as (but not limited to):

Venue hire
PA (sound system) and LX (lighting) hire
Artist catering
Support act fee
Marketing

Below is an example of a more detailed 'costings' for an artist playing at a 200-capacity venue, with a £15 ticket price, on a £350 guarantee vs 80% deal.

(You have probably seen there is a blank example of this in your download pack. You might find this helpful to model some of the different deal structures.)

CAPACITY AND BOX OFFICE POTENTIAL								
	Ticket Price	Capacity Split	Guests permitted above capacity	Guest Holds & Comps	Production Holds	Sellable Capacity	Potential Gross Income	Notes
Level 1 standing	£ 15.00	200	20	20		180	£ 2,700.00	
Total		200	20	20	0	180	£ 2,700.00	

COSTS budgeted for this show			NUMBER OF SHOWS	1
Description	Budget			
1 VENUE HIRE	£ 300.00		FINANCIAL OFFER and Walkout Potential	
2 PRS	£ 94.50		POTENTIAL GROSS INCOME	£ 2,700.00
3 TICKET PRINTING	£ -		VAT	£ 450.00
4 SECURITY			POTENTIAL NET INCOME	£ 2,250.00
5 BOX OFFICE CHARGES	£ 50.00		TOTAL COSTS	£ 1,203.25
6 PRODUCTION OFFICE / INTERNET			BALANCE	£ 1,046.75
7 FIRE / MEDICAL				
8 ELECTRICIAN	£ -			
9 POLICE	£ -		GUARANTEED ARTIST FEE	£ 350.00
10 VENUE INFRASTRUCTURE	£ -			
11 CANCELLATION INSURANCE	£ 33.75		VERSUS	80%
12 PUBLIC LIABILITY INSURANCE	£ -		POTENTIAL ON SELLOUT	£ 837.40
13 STAFF	£ 100.00			
14 MISCELLANEOUS	£ -			
15 NATIONAL ADVERTISING			AVERAGE NET TICKET PRICE	£ 12.50
16 VENUE ADVERTISING RECHARGE	£ -		BREAK EVEN SALES ESTIMATE	119
17 LOCAL ADVERTISING	£ 150.00			
18 POSTER PRINTING	£ 30.00			
19 FLYPOSTING / DISTRIBUTION	£ 50.00		OFFER NOTES:	
20 LEAFLETS / FLYERS	£ 50.00			
21 ONLINE PROMOTION	£ 200.00			
22 ARTWORK / DESIGN	£ 25.00			
23 PR	£ -			
24 TELEVISION / RADIO	£ -			

As you can see from the example, there are substantially more show costs than in our basic example models above. There are also elements in the above that can't be avoided, such as PRS (Performing Rights Society – UK artists' royalties licence contribution) and VAT (value-added tax) which will be deducted from ticket revenue in many UK circumstances.

Generally, show costs will increase as the size of venues you perform in increases, because of higher operating costs, bigger marketing budgets, the venue having more staff to pay, etc. Sometimes (and especially in smaller venues), show costs aren't broken down like the above but are consolidated into one 'agreed costs' figure. It's up to the agent/artist to decide whether these figures are fair in the context of the deal.

Agents will ask for clarification if there are any individual costs that seem unusually high, or if there is something included that they weren't expecting. Some artists/managers will ask to see receipts for evidence of these costs actually being spent. This opens up a whole can of worms around trust, but this is really something that only experience will teach.

I would say that artists in the early stages of their career would do better than to ask for receipts for a £20 'miscellaneous' show cost; hounding the promoter on an amount so trivial would do them more harm than good for future artist-promoter relationships. And I think you've learnt by now how much success in this industry is dependent on relationships.

I believe that if you are playing the right venues (that is to say, the quality, established venues that are on the 'circuit'), and doing so with the right promoters (you did your research earlier I hope?), you are already doing everything right, and your deals will mostly be fair by default. The rest will follow.

Expert Tip:

You will in most cases want to get as much of a guaranteed fee as possible; after all, this is your worst-case scenario 'walkout' fee. That doesn't mean you should forget about the 'backend' deal, however. As we saw in scenario 1 with a flat artist fee, the promoter made almost as much money as the artist because the show sold out. Try to always build in a profit share element to maximise your potential, and pitch for that percentage to be as high as possible. Between 70-80% is common. Go in at 80% rather than 75%, and if you have to, you can come down to 75%.

A Note About Riders

We've all heard the stories about colour-separated M&M rider demands by some artists, but in reality, a good agent understands that riders should always **be reasonable and representative-of-profile for the artist in question**. Many emerging artists fail to understand that aside from giving completely the wrong impression (three cases of beer, three bottles of wine and a bottle of whisky—really?) to professionals in the industry, most of the time they're not about to get their demands, and what they do get, they're paying for themselves regardless out of their fee.

As we've seen from the above typical deals on offer, unless it's a guaranteed-fee deal, show costs are covered before the artist gets any extra payment (and in some cases, before any payment), so the cost of a rider, and/or money for a meal (usually just in the budget as 'catering') is simply added to those costs. In the case of a guaranteed fee, you'll just be offered less money!

Every promoter understands the need to grab a bite to eat before the show, but make life easy on yourself and everyone 'servicing you' (the promoter in this case) and keep it reasonable and realistic, especially in the early stages of your career. Of course, when you become huge and everyone wants a piece of you, you can ask for what you want, and if you don't get it, you don't agree to do the show! Until then, however, and until your 'demand ratio' has flipped, you should opt to actually get the gigs and leave the right impression.

Contracts

Once the deal has been agreed, and the show is confirmed, the agent (or artist) should issue a contract, detailing in writing everything that has been agreed and binding the agreement in law. I'd recommend always sending even a basic one, detailing at the very least:

Names, addresses and contact details of both parties (artist and promoter)
Performance date
Performance venue (and address)
Performance length
Agreed deal with payment terms
Confirmation signature from both parties

Agents spend a lot of their time chasing signed contracts back from promoters. In reality, many tours happen successfully without signed contracts (and on trust alone) but you should always endeavour to have that confirmatory signature, especially while you build up those working relationships.

It's also very common for venues/promoters/festivals to issue their own contracts. When this happens, it's a case of negotiating which contract to actually use, or put into place a combination of the two, summarising the key important points from each party.

Expert Tip:

Have a look at the Musician's Union (UK) standard contract template which you could adapt:

https://www.musiciansunion.org.uk/Files/Contracts/Playing-Live/L1-Hiring-a-band

Key Takeaways from Chapter 7:

- There are various types of deal structure (some being very similar) and every result could be different. Ensure you completely understand the deal that's offered for each show before you confirm.

- Keep an eye on show costs and don't be afraid to ask for clarification on any you're not sure of.

- Be reasonable and realistic with any rider requests. A nice approach is to list the number of people in the travel party who need catering for, any dietary requirements, and just ask to be 'looked after'.

- Always issue a contract for every show you confirm. This will help iron out any issues before, or after the gig.

Chapter 8: Tour Announcements and On-Sale

Once your dates are booked, you'll want to get the shows announced and on sale as soon as possible to ensure a lengthy 'leadup' time. This concept won't be new to you I'm sure, but let's work through it anyway from an agent's perspective.

You'll make the most traction if you announce the run of dates in one go (rather than drip-feeding, show-by-show).

Remember, we want to create a sense of urgency and occasion. This is an exciting time and the opportunity should be capitalised on and exploited to its full potential.

I would suggest picking a date and time a couple of weeks in the future (Thursdays/Fridays around midday work well for announcements) and writing to all the venues/promoters saying that you'll be announcing the tour on this date, and that ticket box offices should be open for sales from this date and time their end. Most venues need at least a week's notice to set up box office and marketing for announcements, but I'd suggest giving them two, to be sure.

Now is also a good time to send them your latest (hi-res) picture and brochure copy/blurb. Remind them to follow and engage with you on social media so that on the day of the announcement, you might have ten promoters/venues (in addition to your publicist/friends/fans) all shouting about your shows and making lots of 'noise'.

Create the occasion, invite people to take part, and enjoy the initial spike of sales.

Make up a great looking 'e-flyer' listing all the dates and share this with the announcement post. On Facebook and Instagram, tag all the venues/promoters in the body of the post so they can see it and share it.

On Twitter, announce the tour in a thread, again ensuring each venue/promoter is tagged.

The aim is to ensure anyone who has an interest is tagged, in the hope that they can then share it far and wide to their network.

Key Takeaways from Chapter 8:

- Always announce a run of dates in one go, with promoters/venues not 'leaking' any show details until the official announcement. This is your one opportunity to create urgency and a spike in initial interest; anything that gets out before it should will weaken the overall impact.

- Social media will come into its own at the announcement; tag as many involved parties as possible and don't be afraid to ask for RT (retweets)!

Chapter 9:
PR, Publicity Material/
Artwork, and Promotion

In this chapter, we'll look at elements that aren't necessarily the responsibility of the agent, but that in many cases the agent has an interest in, or has a role to play as the first point of contact to field requests regarding the shows.

For example, the agent has booked the tour, and is now getting requests from venues for the artist to send posters/flyers. It is the agent's job to ensure this message gets to the artist (or management) and see the job gets done.

PR/Hiring a Publicist

Again, although this book is of course about agents and booking, as we're now more in the 'DIY' mode, and we've already mentioned PR (public relations), I'll quickly give you an agent's view on PR and working with publicists, who are an important member of an artist's team, and whom most agents would suggest recruiting as part of your release/live strategy.

A music publicist's job is essentially to gain as much exposure as they can for the product they are 'servicing'. Whenever you see a full-page spread in a magazine about your favourite artist, or a four-star review of a recent live show in a newspaper, it's most likely there as a result of a publicist's involvement. Hear a song playlisted on mainstream radio or see an artist interviewed on prime-time TV? That will be the work of another form of publicist called a 'plugger'.

Similar to a booking agent, a publicist will maintain a large database of industry contacts, and not only be on friendly terms with the majority, but will have a strong influence on the editors, DJs, head of programming corporations, bloggers, influencers—you name it—that make up most of them.

I'll quickly also clarify that PR is very different to advertising. Advertising is the process of using paid channels to get your message out, and can be bought and placed by anyone. PR is all about editorial features; coverage that looks less like advertising, is more 'spotlight' or recommendation, and gets the message out in a more authentic, brand stamp-of-approval way. Think of PR as reputation management. Most of the text-based features in any mainstream music magazine are the result of a PR campaign. The full-page adverts, very different. You can control advertising, but with PR, you're at the mercy of whoever is writing the feature, and although your publicist will have some influence in shaping the 'story', it's down to the individual who is writing the feature what the outcome (or 2 star review!) looks like.

In terms of your live touring, the PR you'll want will be a mix of physical and online coverage, ideally nationally and regionally. In the best-case scenario, this will be focused around a release, and to do the best job, your publicist will need something like an album to 'hang' the story on: rather than X band is coming to town, it's X band is coming to town, *and they have a fantastic new album out.*

It comes back to having a reason to tour, and a bigger strategy overall, which PR should form an integral part of.

Unlike agents, publicists can be hired, but like agents, they are often very busy people and should be approached in the very early stages (whilst starting to think about release schedules and booking the tour) as to secure their availability.

Not only will a publicist be great for getting news about your record out to the masses (and hopefully landing you some cool reviews in the press), but having someone working on this side of things will also be greatly beneficial to further promote your tour dates, to land some extra bums on seats, and to also help sell the show to the promoters and venues in the first place. If a promoter thinks the artist they're thinking of booking might be featured in the mainstream press as part of a national PR effort, the prospect of booking them suddenly becomes much more attractive.

Publicity Material

A representative from the band should (usually through the agent initially) contact the promoters/venues about publicity material (posters/flyers/artwork) early on after the announcement to form a unified and cohesive marketing plan, and to make sure everyone knows what is expected of them.

While you should certainly make up graphics to share on your online platforms, you should liaise with the venues/promoters about posters; some like to make up their own in their standard 'house style' (and thus might just require a high-quality image and quote from you), whereas others (especially arts centres/theatres) will expect a delivery of actual printed posters and flyers to arrive in the mail at least eight weeks in advance of the show.

After the tour announcement, you should be asking for regular ticket sales updates from each venue/promoter to monitor the sales progress of each show and identify any slow selling ones that might need a bit more attention. This not only shows an interest in how the sales are performing, but also gives them a gentle nudge to ensure they're doing all they can from their side to promote the show.

Expert Tip 1:

I'd recommend having a dedicated page on your website where people can download hi-res pictures, your biography, and some videos. This will save (some) people from having to write to you to ask for them.

Expert Tip 2:

Although collecting sales reports is usually the job of my assistant, I habitually call up promoters directly for sales updates from time to time; it reinforces the fact that I actually care about the show once I've done the deal (after sales service!), allows me to check in with them on a social level, and gives me a chance to tell them about another great tour I've just started booking next year—which *"I'm sure they'd be most interested in!"*

Promotion of the Shows

Again, though the actual promotion of the show lies outside of the responsibility of the agent, it's the agent's role to ensure that the organiser is a) on the case getting the word out about the show, b) has everything they need to do so, and c) is in conversation with the artist or representative so that no wires are crossed and no replicated work is undertaken.

Any good agent will tell you it's a joint effort to promote a show. The promoter is, of course, taking the financial risk and should be working as hard as possible to ensure a busy room on the night, but it's crucial that the artist is doing their bit also; listing the show on their website, promoting it on social media, ensuring their mailing list has been contacted, and crucially, (usually via the agent) has supplied the promoter with the relevant and necessary materials, be it some great pictures and blurb, posters and flyers, or a short video trailer—whatever necessary to help the promoter achieve the best result.

As we have already seen, many show offers are submitted with the risk (and potential) shared between both promoter and artist, but in the early days for artists especially (and/or when their worth is untested) many offers will be structured less around the guarantee element (if there is one) and more around the backend/percentage part of the deal. This way, the more the artist does to promote the show, the higher their resulting fee will likely be. In most cases, it's only when an artist has a proven record of being able to sell a large number of tickets, that the guarantee on offer will be substantial.

My Top Ideas for Pre-Tour Artist Promotional Activities:

- Make a short 'trailer' video for every show. Venues love this. It should be roughly 20 seconds* in length, have some great (ideally live) video footage as the focus element, but with scrolling/popup text listing the town, venue, date, and a couple of good quotes. Send this to every venue/promoter as a video file (not YouTube link) so they can upload it to their website and social media themselves and enjoy the added algorithmic 'organic engagement' benefit of uploaded content, which often performs better than just a link.

- Post one of these videos each day on your social media on the final run-up to the shows. Ensure you are tagging every possible involved party to get as many shares as possible. That's the venue, the promoter and/or organiser, the ticket agent, maybe the local '@whatsonmanchester' or '@visitBrighton' listings account (examples).

- Think about doing a couple of live 'mini gigs' on Facebook and Instagram live (both have slightly different audience bases) to tease your existing fans with the real thing, and persuade potential new ones to come to the main event.

- Create Facebook events for every one of your shows. Ensure the promoter/venue are made co-hosts. If the promoter/venue has created one already, ask to be made a co-host. Either way, check and ensure they're in place.

- Think about doing a social media competition to win tickets to your shows if they help you spread the word by sharing posts/events etc.

- Use smart links to send people to the right places and capture their data at the same time. Check out https://www.linkfire.com.

- Ensure the town, venue name, and ticket link is listed for each show on your website. Make it as easy as possible for people to click-through and go straight to the 'add to basket' stage of the online box office.

- If you have a mailing list, (presuming you've already sent a tour announcement email out to your subscribers) send out a final reminder a couple of weeks before the tour.

- Make an offer to the promoters/venues that you can be available for radio/press interviews if there is anything they'd like to set up. Your publicist will most likely be on the case with this already, but it's good brownie points for the artist to show willing to do everything possible to help get a busy room.

- *20 seconds sounds short, but in the world of social media, it's about right to ensure your audience will watch it long enough to get the message.

Key Takeaways from Chapter 9:

- Though PR and gig promotion lies outside of an agent's remit, they are usually the conduits between parties.

- Not only is having a publicist working the tour a sensible thing to have in terms of product, sales, profile, and exposure, it's also an attractive prospect to potential bookers who might have been previously undecided about offering a booking.

- It's the promoter's job to promote the show, but you as an artist should be working hard to promote it as well. From your online web presence, social media and mailing lists, you have a captive audience, and these should be utilised as much as possible.

Chapter 10: Preparing to Set Out on Tour

The tour is booked, announced, on sale, and hopefully already selling tickets (and, acting as agent, you're checking with the promoters, right?)

Congratulations—you're about to embark on tour.

The work doesn't stop here, however. Aside from actually playing the gigs, there are a few things you can do now to ensure you get the very most from the tour whilst positioning yourself one step ahead of every other band touring at that time.

The Experienced Agent's List of Things to do Before Setting Out on Tour:

- If you haven't already, send a final email reminder about the shows to your mailing list. Include ticket links. Suggest people bring their friends.

- If you have engaged a publicist, ensure you're getting regular progress reports. Liaise often between venue and publicist to ensure any shows that could benefit from a boost in ticket sales are given special attention.

- Contact each promoter/venue at least ten days in advance of your show to finalise the finer details. This is called 'advancing', and regardless of whether the show has been booked yourself, or through an agent, artists (or their managers/tour managers) should always make contact with the organiser before the show. This is a good time to remind them of your understanding of the deal (and perhaps chase a signature for the contract), to ask questions about parking, make them aware of any special requirements you might have (and attach your tech spec), ask if they know of any cheap local accommodation deals (they might offer you a bed!), find out what time doors open, etc. From a promoter's perspective, it's always nice to hear from an artist directly in advance of a show, not only for peace of mind that everything is still on-track, but also to exchange a few words before meeting in person.

- Ensure all your important documents are safe and together. It's also worthwhile thinking about plans in case of emergencies, and making sure that you have as much detail about each show to hand such as mobile phone numbers of promoters/venues.

- This is also a good time to think about guests for each show. You will be able to find out from the organiser how many complimentary tickets are available. Use this facility to invite people who might help your growth to come and enjoy a night out at your gig. Remember to offer them a '+1', and to chat with them (and buy them both a drink) on the night if they turn up!

- Pack your CDs, check you've packed them, and check you've checked you've packed them. The amount of artists that…(I won't even go there).

- Check that all the mundane work is done already so you won't be spending valuable time doing trivial tasks whilst on tour. Have you enough guitar strings? Have you double-checked transport arrangements? Have you prepared forms to collect email addresses for your mailing list at the end of each gig?

- Rehearse thoroughly before the tour. Even if you don't think you need to, do it. A lot of work has gone into this and your show should be as tight and polished as possible.

- Buy a POS card-machine so fans can buy merchandise if they don't have cash!

Key Takeaways from Chapter 10:

- Once the tour is booked, announced, and on sale, you should plan and prepare thoroughly to ensure you're set up to have the best tour experience with minimal problems.

- Ensure the publicist is providing you with progress reports, and that you're getting regular sales updates from each show.

- This is an opportunity to impress the promoters/venues before you've even met. Be intimidatingly professional and pleasant!

- Don't forget your CDs!

Chapter 11: On the Road

Once you hit the road, your work shouldn't stop there. This is the time to exploit every possible opportunity for converting potential new fans, sell as much merchandise as possible, and importantly (from our agent's perspective), impress and make friends with all the promoters and venues (and their teams) who took a chance on you.

My List of On-Tour To-Dos:

- Keep promoting the tour. Be active on social media and promote tomorrow's show today. Share interesting content: venue pictures/posters/video clips from soundcheck/audience pictures/reviews. Be interesting and make your followers feel part of something, feel they're missing out, or feel like they have missed out if they weren't there.

- Shout about each show the next day on social media, tagging the venue/promoter. Thank them, the audience, and say you had a blast.

- Make audience/other musician friends. Remember, your networks of audience and musician friends are as important as your 'industry' ones. Reach out to people you know, invite them to your shows in their area (again, you might be offered a bed for the night!), arrange to go for lunch, have a jam—anything.

- Regardless of whether your tour has been booked yourselves, or through an agent, you want to make sure you're also making friends at every venue you play at. Make sure you introduce yourself to the people involved in helping you do the gig; the promoter, venue manager, the person who actually booked you, the sound engineer, the bar manager etc. Leave a lasting impression before doors have even opened. As we well know by now, the music industry is built on relationships, and if you're remembered as the nice band that went out of their way to say thankyou before the night has even started, you've got yourself a head start.

- Enjoy and sightsee. Every town you play in will have something interesting to learn about or visit, and being out in the fresh air is great for your well-being when you're spending a lot of your time in a car or cooped-up in dark venues.

- Take lots of photos. Even when the tour finishes, the legacy/boasting content from doing it shouldn't, and you should be shouting about it on social media it in the weeks following. Get some good pictures now to use for content once you're back home.

- Build your mailing list. Whenever you sell cds/merch, you should be capturing audience data.

- Remind your audience each night who you are. I'm mainly talking here about festivals, but say your name at the start of your set and repeat it at the end, giving everyone a chance to remember (or find out) who they're watching, and subconsciously absorb your name for the future!

- Tell your audience where you are playing next. They might have loved it so much they'll come again tomorrow when you might be less than an hour's drive away from them. Ask them to tell their friends you're in town.

- Be clear about the deals and the fees you're expecting from each show, and make sure you have copies of contracts on hand just in case of any problems on the day.

- Keep records of how many tickets were sold and monies received from each show; these will be handy ammunition for booking future tours.

- Try to get a quote/reference from the venue or promoter of each of your shows at the end of the night. Providing you did a good job, these will be excellent tools to help when pitching for a subsequent tour, and you might just get a couple that are so good they remain on your biography for years to come.

Key Takeaways from Chapter 11:

- Whilst you're on the road, there are so many things that can be done to leave a great lasting impression, and from the agent's perspective also, that's important; the booking next time should be a breeze because they were 'impressed so much last time'.

- As the adage says, it's an agent's job to get the gig, but it's the artist's job to keep it.

Chapter 12: After the Show and Payments

The gig has finished, and it's been a great night. What is the agent's role now? How do artists get paid?

Though fairly standard in North America, it's less common for artists to be paid on the night in the UK.

If a cash payment has been arranged, after the show the promoter should give the artist (or their representative on the night, a tour manager, for example) a copy of the box office settlement, or reconciliation of box office against versus costs. This will detail all show income and expenditure (remember that show costs should have been agreed in advance) and reveal the resulting fee due to the artist. (This is assuming of course that there is a backend/percentage deal in place; if the deal was a straight guarantee, there would be no need to see the costs and a payment could most likely be given.)

It is common for the agent to receive the money a day or two following the show by bank transfer. This allows the organiser time to have fully received ticket monies from the various outlets they might have been on sale from, and put together the settlement to send to the agent. The agent will then check and query if necessary, before accepting on behalf of the artist and raising an invoice to initiate payment.

Sometimes, a cash payment (for the guarantee element of the fee, for example) can be paid on the night if requested in advance (and possible), but a settlement will still follow from the promoter detailing monies already paid, along with any due extra 'overage' from the percentage break.

Due to the organisational structures behind them, many venues (especially local authority/council-owned/operated theatres and arts centres) cannot make cash payments on the night as a rule, but if cash is preferred by the artists, it's always worth asking the question.

From experience, artists wish to deal with cash on the road less and less these days, and in most cases it's the agent's job to collect and hold the fees for the artist, before paying them across in one payment at the end of the tour (less their commission).

For festivals, it's common to get a booking deposit (or series of deposits) and receive the balance in the days following the event by bank transfer.

Key Takeaways from Chapter 12:

- Establish in advance how and when payment will be made. The advancing stage is a good time to do this.
- Check the box office settlement/reconciliation carefully after every show where there is a backend/percentage deal in place, to ascertain if any extra fee is due. Mistakes can be made, and settlements (and expenditure within) should always be compared with the original offer.

Chapter 13: Final Thoughts

Well, congratulations. You're now basically a fully fledged agent.

I trust you have gained a useful insight into how our world operates and how we approach our work.

As I'm sure you've by now realised, an agent's job is never finished. There is always more hustling to do, more artists to sign, and more commission invoices to draw up!

Hopefully, you have learnt a lot and, dare I say, enjoyed the process.

I wish you every success with the future. If you have any further questions, I'd be delighted to hear from you—read on!

"there is no mission like commission"

Nigel Morton, Moneypenny Agency UK

About the Author

Phil Simpson BA(Hons) F.E.A.A started his journey in the music industry firstly as a performer, playing in bands to fund college and university studies and having as much fun organising the gigs as actually playing them.

After graduating with a degree in Creative Music Technology from the University of Hull, UK in 2008, Phil continued promoting shows with increasingly bigger artists and realised he wanted to be the person 'on the other end of the phone', and closer to the 'real' music industry; working directly with the artists and building their careers.

Whilst working as Events Assistant at The Basement music venue in York, UK, and teaching guitar lessons part-time, he took on a work experience placement under the direction of Chris Wade at the Adastra agency. Phil was subsequently offered a full-time job with the company in 2009, and went on to represent a roster of sixteen artists, some of which he still works with to this day.

In 2012, Phil set up his own company, Regent Music; a boutique, full-service booking agency that quickly went on to represent some of the biggest names in the Acoustic/Folk/World genres.

In 2014, he merged Regent Music with another agency, GPS Music, operated by independent booking agent Graham Smout. Together, they further built the agency up, and it became well known for its great reputation and enviable roster of over twenty-five artists.

In 2016, Phil merged Regent Music with his old employer, the Adastra agency, to create Strada Music LLP. The agency now represents over eighty artists in the Acoustic, Roots, Folk, World and Pop genres and is one of the largest independent agencies of its kind in the Europe.

Phil was awarded a fellowship by the Entertainment Agents' Association in 2019.

Alongside booking, Phil also runs a successful artist mentorship scheme, and in his spare time, enjoys writing non-fiction, writing, playing, and performing music himself, spending time with his wife and son, and walking his collie-lurcher cross Howie.

Connect with Phil on Instagram @agent_phil_simpson.

Or by email: info@touringartiststoolkit.com

Learn more about Phil's mentorship schemes, and keep up to date with all the latest news at The Touring Artist's Toolkit:

www.touringartiststoolkit.com

The Big Glossary

They say everyone is 'winging it' in this game; there is no standard career path, nor is there any formal qualification. We learn by doing, and anyone who professes to know everything in this field is probably best avoided anyway. There are no silly questions. Below is an extensive list detailing some of the terms used in this book, but also some from other areas of the industry which you may well encounter on your journey.

+1 – a name 'plus one' on the guestlist.

A&R – stands for 'Artist and Repertoire'; the talent-seeking/signing process.

ADMAT – (Advertising Material) – refers to an artist's editable gig poster template.

ADVANCING – pre-show confirmation of the finer details from artist/management.

ARTIST(s) – performer(s); solo, ensemble, band.

BACKEND – the 'bonus' element of a deal structure; i.e. vs 75% door split.

BILL – line up/list of artists performing at an event.

BOOKER – the person who books the artists for events; often the 'talent buyer'.

BOOKING AGENT – you hopefully know this one by now!

BOX OFFICE – the physical or online platform where tickets are sold.

BOX OFFICE RECONCILIATION (SEE SETTLEMENT)

BUY-OUT – a per-person amount of sustenance money given to the artist by the promoter.

CALL – in reference to deal structures, is an allocated portion of fee agreed in advance.

CAMPAIGN – see PR; also a period of focus/emphasis, maybe a new album cycle etc.

COMPS – usually referring to complimentary tickets on a guestlist.

CONTRACT – legally enforceable commitment document between artist and buyer.

COPY – edited band blurb/biography, used in brochures/on websites to sell the show.

COSTINGS – a breakdown of show costs, usually accompanying the offer.

COVERS – songs written by persons other than the artist. '*Covering other peoples' songs.*'

CROWDFUNDING – directly raising money from fans or 'supporters'.

CURFEW – time which building should be exited, or when music stopped by (**NOISE**).

CYCLE – (usually 'album cycle') the duration of the period/campaign around a new album.

EP – 'Extended Play'; a release of around five songs.

EPK – Electronic Press Kit. A central online point for images, bio, music/video, links etc.

EXCLUSIVITY – see RADIUS CLAUSE.

FOH – Front of House. Either a FOH sound engineer, or referring to the space 'out front'.

GROSS BOX OFFICE – revenue / figure stating the value of a number of tickets sold.

GUESTLIST – list of pre-authorised persons who can come into the show for free.

HARD TICKET – where the draw of the headline band is relied on.

HEADLINER – the foremost billed artist; not necessarily last to perform.

HOLDS – the act of 'holding' or 'pencilling' dates with venues until you're able to confirm.

LOAD IN – the time the artist should arrive to unload equipment, before soundcheck.

LEAD-IN – a 'run up' to/wait for something; record release, a tour, or show.

LP – 'Long Play'; becoming archaic, but another word for an album/full-length release.

LX – short for lighting/lights.

MANAGER – an artist's main representative and central liaison point for their team.

MEDIA – usually referring to the press/online.

MERCH – short for saleable merchandise; CDs, t-shirts, badges etc.

NET BOX OFFICE (NBO) – box office revenue less costs.

ONE-OFF – a single show/not part of a bigger run of dates.

ONE SHEET – One page detailing everything about the artist; pic, bio, quotes, links etc.

OPENER – an opening, or support act.

OVERAGE – the 'extra'% split money an artist might receive on top of a guaranteed fee.

PA – Public Address, or 'PA system'/amplification for the whole sound of the artist.

PAPERING THE HOUSE – where tickets are given away because a show hasn't sold.

PENCILS – see HOLDS.

PER DIEM – 'per day'; an artist's daily allocated expense money whilst on tour.

PLUGGER – a member of the PR team which 'plugs' a product, usually to TV/Radio.

PPL – the UK's collection society for sound recording royalties known as 'mechanicals.'

PR – Public Relations; the artist's 'relationship' with the public, via the media.

PRIMARY MARKET – the towns/cities with the biggest potential audience.

PROMOTER – a show organiser, or talent buyer. Often the booker.

PROMOTION – the advertising, raising awareness of a show. Done by the promoter.

PRS – the UK's agency for artists' live performance royalties.

PUBLICIST – someone who drives a PR campaign, seeks promotional press coverage.

PUBLISHER – administers and represents the works and rights of songwriters.

RADIUS CLAUSE – booking exclusivity within a stated geographic radius & timeframe.

RECORD LABEL – an organisation which represents and releases an artist's records.

RELEASE – referring to the launch or distribution of a product such as an album.

RIDER – 'rides' with the contract; lists extra items (catering or tech) to be supplied.

ROUTING – see Chapter 6!

SINGLE – a track/recording release; often ahead of, featured on, an upcoming album.

SECONDARY MARKET – towns/cities not initially considered to have best potential.

SETTLEMENT – an after-show reconciliation of costs vs income.

SOFT TICKET SHOW – where event itself is main attraction; i.e. a festival.

SOUND CHECK – an opportunity to test and balance sound levels before the performance.

SPLIT or **BREAK POINT** – the ticket sales figure where a backend % bonus kicks in.

SYNC – placement (synchronisation) of music to moving pictures such as adverts, films etc.

TALENT BUYER – individual who pays artists to perform. Sometimes 'Purchaser'.

TECH SPEC – document outlining the artist's stage set up/instrumentation/requirements.

TERTIARY MARKET – towns/cities with least potential or 'untested' areas.

TM – short for Tour Manager. An artist's on-tour assistant/representative/logistics.

TRAVEL PARTY – the total number of people on the road. Artists, crew, TM etc.

UNDERPLAY – a show with expected sell-out, as capacity is lower than expected audience.

VENUE – place or establishment which facilitates a performance.

WALK-UP – gig attendees who 'walk up' to the show without having advance tickets.

Recommended Resources

I've always had a thirst for knowledge and believe it's healthy to regularly reevaluate what we do, why we do it, and look at the ways in which we can improve. Even if you're reading about what you already know, it's often useful just to hear someone else's point of view. I've put together a few resources below I've enjoyed over the years that are all worth your time.

The Unsigned Guide

https://www.theunsignedguide.com
Lots of useful reading on this popular blog, aside from their ever-popular guide.

Music Business Worldwide

https://www.musicbusinessworldwide.com/
A great place to find out all the latest music industry news.

Music ThinkTank

http://www.musicthinktank.com
Lots of great articles here across a whole spectrum of the industry, written by some great contributors. I read this a lot.

Ari's Take

https://aristake.com
Ari's Take is a fantastic resource for the independent musician. You could (and I recommend you do) spend hours absorbing the wealth of great information available here.

Book: **All You Need to Know About the Music Business by Donald S. Passman**.

A comprehensive read covering all aspects of the industry. An industry standard.

Book: **Bill Graham Presents by Graham Greenfield.**

An inspiring reflection on the life of legendary concert promoter Bill Graham. Full of great Rock n' Roll stories about the 'old days' of the music industry.

Video: **Randy Pausch's 'Last Lecture'- Really Achieving Your Childhood Dreams.**

Highly recommended life-affirming viewing.

"Experience is what you get when you didn't get what you wanted"

"Brick walls are there for a reason; they give us a chance to prove how badly we want something…these walls can be climbed by people who dare to fight back and don't accept defeat."

https://youtu.be/ji5_MqicxSo

Podcast: **Promoter 101**

Interviews with some of the biggest players in the music industry; agents, promoters, publicists, you name it. A great listen.

http://www.promoter101.net/podcast

Printed in Great Britain
by Amazon

19215624R10058